# Let's Explore
# France

by Elle Parkes

LERNER PUBLICATIONS ◆ MINNEAPOLIS

**Note to Educators:**

Throughout this book, you'll find critical thinking questions. These can be used to engage young readers in thinking critically about the topic and in using the text and photos to do so.

Lerner Publications Company
A division of Lerner Publishing Group, Inc.
241 First Avenue North
Minneapolis, MN 55401 USA

For reading levels and more information, look up this title at www.lernerbooks.com.

**Library of Congress Cataloging-in-Publication Data**

Names: Parkes, Elle, author.
Title: Let's explore France / by Elle Parkes.
Description: Minneapolis : Lerner Publications, [2018] | Series: Bumba books--Let's explore countries | Audience: K to grade 3.
  | Includes bibliographical references and index.
Identifiers: LCCN 2016042314 (print) | LCCN 2016043468 (ebook) | ISBN 9781512433661 (library bound : alkaline paper) |
  ISBN 9781512455588 (paperback : alkaline paper) | ISBN 9781512450422 (eb pdf)
Subjects: LCSH: France—Juvenile literature.
Classification: LCC DC17 .P37 2018 (print) | LCC DC17 (ebook) | DDC 944—dc23

LC record available at https://lccn.loc.gov/2016042314

Manufactured in the United States of America
1 – CG – 7/15/17

LERNER
SOURCE

Expand learning beyond the printed book. Download free, complementary educational resources for this book from our website, www.lerneresource.com.

# Table of
# Contents

# A Visit to France

France is a country.

It is in Europe.

It is between the ocean and the sea.

5

France has flat plains.

It has tall mountains.

Forests cover other areas.

What do you think grows on France's plains?

Deer live in the forests.

Rabbits live there too.

Many birds fly through France.

Flamingos live in southern France.

France has big cities.

Paris is the largest city.

Many people live there.

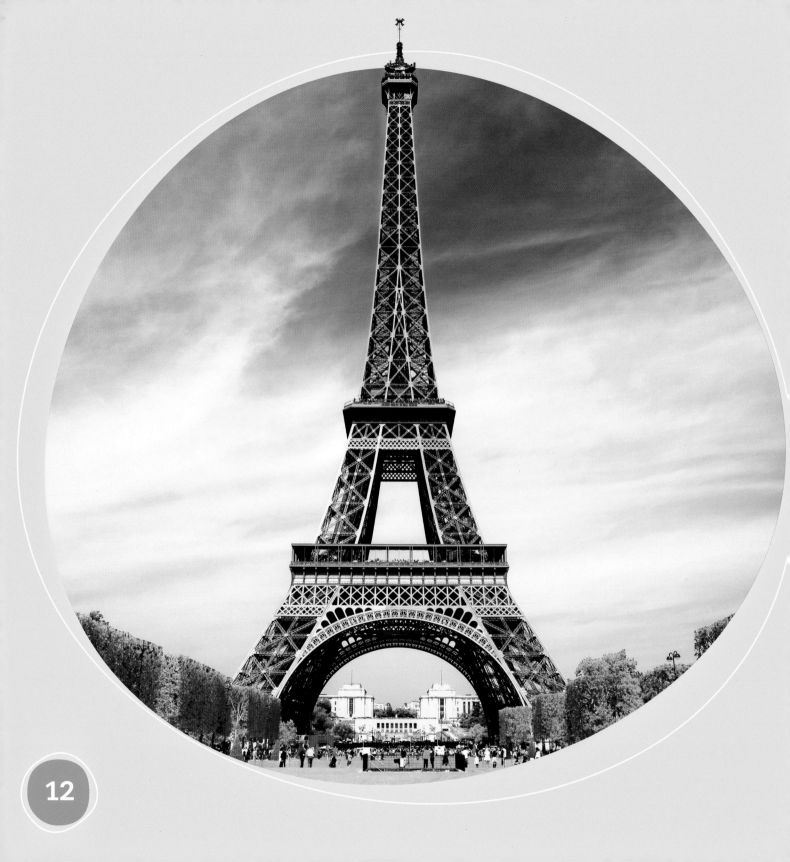

People like to visit France.

They go to museums.

They see the Eiffel Tower in Paris.

Why do you think people like to visit France?

The Arc de Triomphe is also in Paris.

It is a popular thing to see.

Cheese is a top French food. There are many kinds of cheese. People eat it with different meats.

What other foods do you think the French eat with cheese?

Biking is a fun activity to do in France.

Rock climbing is also popular.

France is a beautiful country.

There are many things

to see.

Would you like to go

to France?

# Map of France

Paris

France

ocean

mountains

sea

# Picture Glossary

**flamingos**

large, pink birds with long necks and long legs

**forests**

large areas covered with full-grown trees

**museums**

places where art and objects from the past are on display

**plains**

big, flat pieces of land

# Read More

Borgert-Spaniol, Megan. *Flamingos*. Minneapolis: Bellwether, 2015.

Gilbert, Sara. *French Food*. Mankato, MN: Creative Education, 2015.

Parkes, Elle. *Let's Explore Egypt*. Minneapolis: Lerner Publications, 2018.

# Index

## Photo Credits